D0801194

AN ARROW
AGAINST ALL TYRANTS

First published in 1646

This edition published by Canbury Press in 2020

Canbury Press
Kingston upon Thames, Surrey, United Kingdom

Printed and bound in Great Britain
by CPI Group (UK) Ltd, Croydon

All rights reserved © Ian Gadd has asserted his
right to be identified as the author of the introduction
to this work in accordance with Section 77 of the
Copyright, Designs and Patents Act 1988

This is a work of non-fiction.

Typeset by Canbury Press

ISBN
Paperback: 978-1-912454-57-0
Ebook: 978-1-912454-58-7
PDF: 978-1-912454-59-4

www.canburypress.com
Telling the real story since 2013

AN ARROW

AGAINST ALL TYRANTS

RICHARD OVERTON

Introduction

In October 1646, somewhere on the streets of London, the bookseller George Thomason picked up a scruffily printed work entitled *An Arrow Against all Tyrants and Tyranny* by Richard Overton (*fl.* 1640-63) and, as was his habit, noted the date of his latest acquisition on its title-page. Thomason had been systematically collecting all sorts of printed items since 1640 and *An Arrow* was just the latest example of what he and his contemporaries would have called a pamphlet — a word that, of course, still has currency today but that lacks much of the potency and meaning that it had for Overton's first readers.

First of all, a pamphlet was not a book. This may seem a curious thing to say, especially as you're currently holding this book in your hands, but a 17th Century reader would have understood the distinction. For a start, a pamphlet was not bound. Many printed works in England in this period were sold unbound — as folded, printed sheets — in the expectation that a purchaser would get them bound, but some kinds of printed items, including pamphlets, were never intended for binding. Instead, a pamphlet like *An Arrow* would have been 'stab stitched': simply held together by coarse thread that had been stabbed through the left-hand margin when the pamphlet was closed. In contrast to the careful, precise, and hidden sewing of a book binding, stab-stitching signalled a pamphlet's sense of urgency and directness — and also its likely ephemerality.

Pamphlets were also relatively short: some might be only a few pages long, others might stretch beyond a few dozen. *An Arrow* is 20 pages, with each copy made up of two and a half printed sheets, each folded twice. Finally, English printing was not yet near the quality of

French or Italian practice and pamphlets were often particularly poorly printed, with ink-blots, uneven impressions, damaged type, and typos. After all, pamphlets were printed at speed, at relatively low cost, and, in the 1640s especially, often in secret.

None of this means that pamphlets were simple, straightforward, or careless in their contents. They could be complex, opaque, playful, provocative, and knowing. Their tone was direct, at times declamatory (such as when Overton writes 'Be awakened, arise and consider their oppressions and encroachments'), and even when they were anonymous, the authorial voice was always distinctive and polemical. They aimed to argue and persuade, to expose and mock, and, at times, to incite. They existed in a densely textual world, in dialogue with other pamphlets (often explicitly) and frequently quoted from texts elsewhere: *An Arrow*, for example, quotes Magna Carta, parliamentary statute, and legal precedent as well as the daily records of Parliament itself.

They could be performative, too. *An Arrow* includes not only a public letter to one of the most outspoken MPs of the day, Henry Marten (who would soon become a Leveller sympathiser), but also a petition to Parliament for Overton's own release from prison. They were mercurial in form — *An Arrow* mixes letter, excerpts, and petitions — and often self-aware. On its title-page *An Arrow* not only mocks the official licensing system with its self-declared 'IMPRIMATUR' ('let it be printed') but also revels in a fictional imprint:

> *Printed at the backside of the Cyclopian Mountains by Martin Claw-Clergy, Printer to the reverend Assembly of Divines, and are to be sould at the signe of Subjects Liberty, right opposite to persecuting Court.*

This echoed Overton's *Nativity of Sir John Presbyter* (1645) that claimed it had been printed 'on the back-side of Cyclopian mountains' and the imprint of an earlier pamphlet, *A Dreame: Or Newes from Hell* (1641), 'Printed in Sicilia on the back-side of the Cyclopean mountaines', which may also have had an Overton connection.

Pamphlets were emphatically topical, speaking to the immediate political, religious, or cultural moment. Specific dates mattered: Overton dates his letter and postscript to 25th September and 12th October 1646, and from Thomason's own dating of his copy, we know that *An Arrow* was circulating practically immediately. Printing and distribution needed to be speedy, especially at a time of such political and religious uncertainty: readers depended on pamphlets to be current. History tends to flatten the sequencing of pamphlets and other topical writings but the date of publication mattered. Printers might hasten or delay publication in order to incorporate new developments or to coincide with other important events, but once the pamphlet was printed, a multitude of street-sellers could distribute it across London in hours. Little wonder that a reader in 1642 could wryly remark that 'these little pamphlets... were so many thieves that had stolen my money before I was aware of them.'

We don't know exactly where in London *An Arrow* was printed, who printed it, who paid for its publication, how many copies were printed, or how much it cost a reader to buy. We do know, though, that pamphlets were cheap, selling for pennies, and may even have been given away. They found a ready readership in London, where at times well over half of adult men could read, and where reading out loud was a common social practice. Even so, publishing a printed work for sale was (and remains) a risky business: no one could know how well or badly one might fare in the marketplace. Given the cost of paper, ink, and labour, it made sense to print at least a few hundred copies to stand a chance of recouping an investment, but printing too many could mean losses if copies remained unsold — and an unsold pamphlet quickly became an unsellable one. The immediacy of the market meant that a publisher would discover if they'd printed the right number of copies in a matter of days, if not hours. Unless a pamphlet generated exceptional demand there was little appetite to reprint, because events – and readers — had a habit of moving on.

The centre of London's book trade in the 1640s was, as it had been for over a century, just to the north-east of St Paul's Cathedral, but there were bookshops and presses, legal and illegal, across London as well as many 'hawkers' and 'mercuries' selling directly in the street. Printing and bookselling were regulated and policed, albeit sporadically and often ineffectually, by two entities. The first was London's book trade guild, the Stationers' Company, to whom Thomason belonged. Many of its members made livelihoods from printing and selling pamphlets. The second was the Parliamentary government, which reestablished the pre-Reformation system of licensing in 1643 (prompting Milton's famous *Areopagitica*) and sought to suppress illicit works and presses, often co-opting the Company's officers for that purpose (and subsequently berating them for their inadequacies).

One underground press, run by Richard Overton himself, had been printing pamphlets since September 1644. Both Parliament and the Stationers' Company had attempted to locate it — a Company-run raid in June 1646 seized equipment and pamphlets, but no personnel. Finally in August, both press and printer were tracked down to Southwark. It was while in prison, two months later, that Overton wrote *An Arrow* justifying his political views and petitioning for his release (although this would not come for another year). It was printed immediately, on an unknown press by an unknown printer, and confirmed what every reader in 1640s London knew: that the thoughts in pamphlets — unlike the men who wrote and printed them — could not be contained.

Ian Gadd

Professor of English Literature, Bath Spa University

Further reading

- David R. Adams, 'The Secret Printing and Publishing Career of Richard Overton the Leveller, 1644–46', *The Library* (2010)
- *The Oxford History of Popular Print Culture: Cheap Print in Britain and Ireland to* 1660, ed. by Joad Raymond (2011)
- Jason Peacey, 'News, Pamphlets, and Public Opinion', in *The Oxford Handbook of Literature and the English Revolution*, ed. by Laura Lunger Knoppers (2012)

A Pamphlet in Four Parts

Richard Overton wrote *An Arrow Against all Tyrants and Tyranny* while imprisoned indefinitely in Newgate, London, having been arrested in August 1646 for printing 'scandalous things' against the House of Lords. The pamphlet comprises four parts: a lengthy and complex letter, dated 25 September, from Overton to Henry Marten, an MP sympathetic to his cause; an undated petition from Overton to the House of Commons protesting against his arrest on the grounds that the House of Lords had exceeded its authority; an excerpt from the House of Lords' records for 11 August, reporting Overton's arrest and imprisonment; and a 'Postscript', again addressed to Marten, dated 12 October. Overton remained in prison until September 1647.

An Arrow

Against All Tyrants

Richard Overton

12 October 1646

An arrow against all tyrants and tyranny, shot from the prison of Newgate into the prerogative bowels of the arbitrary House of Lords, and all other usurpers and tyrants whatsoever

By Richard Overton

Prerogative archer to the arbitrary House of Lords, their prisoner in Newgate, for the just and legal properties, rights and freedoms of the Commons of England. Sent by way of a letter from him, to Mr Henry Marten, a member of the House of Commons

Imprimatur Rectat Justitia

Printed at the backside of the Cyclopian Mountains, by Martin Claw-Clergy, printer to the reverend Assembly of Divines, and are to be sold at the sign of the Subject's Liberty, right opposite to Persecuting Court. 1646

Sir,

To every individual in nature is given an individual property by nature not to be invaded or usurped by any. For every one, as he is himself, so he has a self-propriety, else could he not be himself; and of this no second may presume to deprive any of without manifest violation and affront to the very principles of nature and of the rules of equity and justice between man and man. Mine and thine cannot be, except this be: no man has power over my rights and liberties, and I over no man's. I may be but an individual, enjoy myself and my self-propriety and may write myself no more than my self, or presume any further; if I do, I am an encroacher and an invader upon another man's right — to which I have no right. For by natural birth all men are equally and alike born to like propriety, liberty and freedom; and as we are delivered of God by the hand of nature into this world, every one with a natural, innate freedom and propriety — as it were writ in the table of every man's heart, never to be obliterated — even so are we to live, everyone equally and alike to enjoy his birthright and privilege; even all whereof God by nature has made him free.

And this by nature everyone desires, aims at and requires; for no man naturally would be befooled of his liberty by his neighbour's craft or enslaved by his neighbour's might. For it is nature's instinct to preserve itself from all things hurtful and obnoxious; and this in nature is granted of all to be most reasonable, equal and just: not to be rooted out of the kind, even of equal duration with the creature. And from this fountain or root all just human powers take their original — not immediately from God (as kings usually plead their prerogative) but mediately by the hand of nature, as from the represented to the representers. For originally God has implanted them in the creature, and from the creature those powers immediately proceed and no further. And no more may be communicated than stands for the better being, weal, or safety thereof. And this is man's prerogative and no further; so much and no more may be given or received thereof: even so much as is conducent to a better being, more safety and freedom, and no more. He that gives more, sins against his own flesh; and he that takes more is a thief and robber to his kind — every man by nature being a king, priest and prophet in his own natural circuit and compass, whereof no second may partake but by deputation, commission, and free consent from him whose natural right and freedom it is.

And thus sir and no otherwise are you instated into your sovereign capacity for the free people of this nation. For their better being, discipline, government, propriety and safety have each of them communicated so much unto you (their chosen ones) of their natural rights and powers, that you might thereby become their absolute commissioners and lawful deputies, but no more: and that by contraction of those their several individual communications conferred upon and united in you, you alone might become their own natural, proper, sovereign power, therewith singly and only empowered for their several weals, safeties and freedoms, and no otherwise. For as by nature no man may abuse, beat, torment, or afflict himself, so by nature no man may give that power to another, seeing he may not do it himself; for no more can be communicated from the general than is included in the particulars whereof the general is compounded.

So that such, so deputed, are to the general no otherwise than as a school-master to a particular, to this or that man's family. For as such an one's mastership, ordering and regulating power is but by deputation, and that *ad bene placitum* and may be removed at the parents' or headmaster's pleasure upon neglect or abuse thereof, and be conferred upon another (no parents ever giving such an absolute unlimited power to such over their children as to do to them as they list, and not to be retracted, controlled, or restrained in their exorbitances), even so and no otherwise is it with you our deputies in respect of the general is in vain for you to think you have power over us to save us or destroy us at your pleasure, to do with us as you list, be it for our weal or be it for our woe, and not be enjoined in mercy to the one or questioned in justice for the other. For the edge of your own arguments against the king in this kind may be turned upon yourselves. For if for the safety of the people he might in equity be opposed by you in his tyrannies, oppressions and cruelties, even so may you by the same rule of right reason be opposed by the people in general in the like cases of destruction and ruin by you upon them; for the safety of the people is the sovereign law, to which all must become subject, and for the which all powers human are ordained by them; for tyranny, oppression and cruelty whatsoever, and in whomsoever, is in itself unnatural, illegal, yea absolutely anti-magisterial; for it is even destructive to all human civil society, and therefore resistible.

Now sir, the commons of this nation, having empowered their body representative (whereof you are one) with their own absolute sovereignty, thereby authoritatively and legally to remove from amongst them all oppressions and tyrannies, oppressors and tyrants — how great soever in name, place, or dignity — and to protect, safeguard and defend them from all such unnatural monsters, vipers and pests, bred of corruption or which are entrusted amongst them; and as much as in them lies to prevent all such for the future. And to that end you have been assisted with our lives and fortunes most liberally and freely with most victorious and happy success, whereby your arms are strengthened with our might, that now you may make us all happy within the confines of this nation if you please. And therefore sir, in reason, equity and justice we deserve no less at your hands. And (sir) let it not seem strange unto you that we are thus bold with you for our own.

For by nature we are the sons of Adam, and from him have legitimately derived a natural propriety, right and freedom, which only we require. And how in equity you can deny us we cannot see. It is but the just rights and prerogative of mankind (whereunto the people of England are heirs apparent as well as other nations) which we desire; and sure you will not deny it us, that we may be men and live like men. If you do, it will be as little safe for yourselves and posterity as for us and our posterity. For sir, look: what bondage, thraldom, or tyranny soever you settle upon us, you certainly, or your posterity will taste of the dregs. If by your present policy and (abused) might, you chance to award it from yourselves in particular, yet your posterity — do what you can — will be liable to the hazard thereof.

And therefore sir we desire your help for your own sakes as well as for ourselves, chiefly for the removal of two most insufferable evils daily encroaching and increasing upon us, portending and threatening inevitable destruction and confusion of yourselves, of us, and of all our posterities: namely the encroachments and usurpations of the House of Lords over the commons' liberties and freedoms, together with the barbarous, inhuman, blood-thirsty desires and endeavours of the Presbyterian clergy.

For the first, namely the exorbitances of the Lords: they are to such an height aspired, that contrary to all precedents, the free commoners of England are imprisoned, fined and condemned by them (their incompetent, illegal, unequal, improper judges) against the express letter of Magna Carta chapter 29 (so often urged and used): that no free man of England 'shall be passed upon, tried, or condemned, but by the lawful judgement of his equals, or by the law of the land', which, as says Sir Edward Coke in his exposition of Magna Carta, p. 28, last line, is *per pares*, by his peers, that is, by his equals'. And page 46, branches 1, 2 and 5, in these words:

1. That no man be taken or imprisoned, but *per legem terrae*, that is by the common law, statute law, or custom of England. For these words, *per legem terrae* being towards the end of this chapter, do refer to all the pretended matters in this chapter; and this has the first place, because the liberty of a man's person is more precious to him than all the rest that follow; and therefore it is great reason that he should by law be relieved therein, if he be wronged, as hereafter shall be showed.

2. No man shall be disseised, that is, put out of seisin, or dispossessed of his freehold (that is, lands or livelihood) or of his liberties or free customs (that is, of such franchises and freedoms, and free customs, as belong to him by his free birthright) unless it be by the lawful judgement, that

is verdict of his equals (that is of men of his own condition) or by the law of the land (that is, to speak it once for all) by the due course and processes of law.

3. No man shall be in any sort destroyed unless it be by the verdict of his equals or according to the law of the land.

And, chapter 29 of Magna Carta, it is said, *secundum legem et consuetudinem Angliae,* after the law and custom of England, *non regis Angliae* not of the king of England, lest it might be thought to bind the king only, *nec populi Angliae,* not the people of England, but that the law might tend to all, it is said, *per legem terra,* by the law of the land.

Against this ancient and fundamental law, and in the very face thereof, says Sir Edward Coke, he found an act of the parliament made in the 11 Hen. VII cap. 3: that as well Justices of the Peace, without any finding or presentment by the verdict of twelve men, upon the bare information for the king before them, should have full power and authority by their discretions to hear and determine all offences and contempts committed or done by any person or persons against the form, ordinance, and effect of any statute made and not repealed. By colour of which act, shaking this fundamental law, it is not credible (says he) what horrible oppressions and exactions — to the undoing of infinite numbers of people — were committed by Sir Richard Empson, Knight, and Edmund Dudley, being Justices of the Peace through England; and upon this unjust and injurious act (as commonly in the like cases it falls out) a new office was erected, and they made Masters of the King's Forfeitures.

But at the parliament held in 1 Hen. VIII (cap. 6), this Act of Henry VII is recited, made void and repealed; and the reason thereof is yielded: for that by force of the said act it was manifestly known that many sinister, crafty, and forged informations had been pursued against divers of the king's subjects, to their great damage and unspeakable vexation — a thing most frequent and usual at this day and in these times — the ill success whereof, together with the most fearful end of these great oppressors, should deter others from committing the like and should admonish parliaments in the future, that instead of this ordinary and precious trial *per legem terra* they bring not in an absolute and partial trial by discretion.

And to this end the judgement upon Simon de Beresford, a commoner, in the fourth year of Edward III's reign, is an excellent precedent for these times (as is to be seen upon record in the Tower in the second roll of parliament held the same year of the said king and delivered into the Chancery by Henry de Edenston, Clerk of the Parliament) — for that the said Simon de Beresford having counselled, aided and assisted Roger de Mortimer to the murder of the father of the said king, the king commanded the earls and barons in the said parliament assembled to give right and lawful judgement unto the said Simon de Beresford. But the earls, barons and peers came before the lord the king in the same parliament and said with one voice that the aforesaid Simon was not their peer or equal, wherefore they were not bound to judge him as a peer of the land. Yet notwithstanding all this, the earls, barons and peers (being over-swayed by the king) did award and adjudge (as judges of parliament, by the assent of the king in the said parliament) that the said Simon as a traitor and enemy of the realm should be hanged and drawn; and execution accordingly was done. But as by the said roll appears, it was by full parliament condemned and adjudged as illegal, and as a precedent not to be drawn into example. The words of the said roll are these, viz.

And it is assented and agreed by our lord the king and all the grandees in full parliament: that albeit the said peers as judges in full parliament took upon them in presence of our lord the king to make and give the said judgement by the assent of the king upon some of them that were not their peers (to wit commoners) and by reason of the murder of the liege lord, and destruction of him which was so near of the blood royal and the king's father; that therefore the said peers which now are, or the peers which shall be for the time to come, be not bound or charged to give judgement upon others than upon their peers, nor shall do it; but of that for ever be discharged and acquitted; and that the aforesaid judgement now given be not drawn into example or consequent for the time to come, by which the said peers may be charged hereafter to judge others than their peers, being against the law of the land, if any such case happen, which God defend.

Agrees with the Record. William Collet.

But notwithstanding all this our lords in parliament take upon them as judges in parliament to pass judgement and sentence (even of themselves) upon the commoners which are not their peers — and that to fining, imprisonment, etc. And this doth not only content them, but they even send forth their armed men, and beset, invade, assault their houses and persons in a warlike manner and take what plunder they please, before so much as any of their pretended, illegal warrants be showed — as was lately upon 11 August 1646 perpetrated against me and mine, which was more than the king himself by his legal prerogative ever could do. For neither by verbal commands or commissions under the Great Seal of England could he ever give any lawful authority to any general, captain or person whatsoever, without legal trial and conviction, forcibly to assault, rob, spoil or imprison any of the free commoners of England. And in case any free commoner by such his illegal commissions, orders or warrants, before they be lawfully convicted, should be assaulted, spoiled, plundered, imprisoned, etc., in such cases his agents and ministers ought to be proceeded against, resisted, apprehended, indicted and condemned (notwithstanding such commissions) as trespassers, thieves, burglars, felons, murderers, both by statute and common law, as is enacted and resolved by Magna Carta, cap. 29; 15 Eliz. 3 stat. 1. caps. 1, 2, 3; 42 Eliz. 5 cap. 1, 3; 28 Eliz. 1 Artic. sup. chartas, cap. 2; 4 Eliz. 3 cap. 4; 5 Eliz. 3 cap. 2; 24 Eliz. 3 cap. 1; 2 Rich II cap. 7; 5 Rich. II cap. 5; 1 Hen V cap. 6; 11 Hen II caps. 1-6; 24 Hen. VIII cap. 5; 21 James. cap. 3.

And if the king himself have not this arbitrary power, much less may his peers or companions, the lords, over the free commons of England. And therefore notwithstanding such illegal censures and warrants either of king or of Lords (no legal conviction being made) the persons invaded and assaulted by such open force of arms may lawfully arm themselves, fortify their houses (which are their castles in the judgement of the law) against them; yea, disarm, beat, wound, repress and kill them in their just necessary defence of their own persons, houses, goods, wives and families, and not be guilty of the least offence — as is expressly resolved by the Statute of 21 Edw. de malefactoribus in parcis; by 24 Hen. VIII cap. 5; 11 Hen. VI cap. 16; 14 Hen. VI cap. 24; 35 Hen. VI cap. 12; Edward IV cap. 6.

And therefore (sir) as even by nature and by the law of the land I was bound, I denied subjection to these lords and their arbitrary creatures thus by open force invading and assaulting my house, person, etc. — no legal conviction preceding, or warrant then shown. But and if they had brought and shown a thousand such warrants, they had all been illegal, antimagisterial and void in this case; for they have no legal power in that kind, no more than the king, but such their actions are utterly condemned and expressly forbidden by the law. Why therefore should you of the representative body sit still and suffer these lords thus to devour both us and our laws?

Be awakened, arise and consider their oppressions and encroachments and stop their lordships in their ambitious career. For they do not cease only here, but they soar higher and higher and now they are become arrogators to themselves of the natural sovereignty the represented have conveyed and issued to their proper representers. They even challenge to themselves the title of the supremest court of judicature in the land — as was claimed by the Lord Hunsden when I was before them, which you may see more at large in a printed letter published under my name, entitled *A defiance against all arbitrary usurpations* — which challenge of his (I think I may be bold to assert) was a most illegal, anti-parliamentary, audacious presumption, and might better be pleaded and challenged by the king singly than by all those lords in a distinction from the Commons. But it is more than may be granted to the king himself; for the parliament, and the whole kingdom whom it represents, is truly and properly the highest supreme power of all others — yea above the king himself.

And therefore much more above the Lords. For they can question, cancel, disannul and utterly revoke the king's own royal charters, writs, commissions, patents, etc., though ratified with the Great Seal — even against his personal will, as is evident by their late abrogation of sundry patents, commissions, writs, charters, loan, ship-money etc. Yea the body representative have power to enlarge or retract the very prerogative of the king, as the Statute *de prerog. Reg.* and the parliament roll of I Hen. IV, num. 18. doth evidence; and therefore their power is larger and higher than the king's; and if above the king's, much more above the Lords', who are subordinate to the king. And if the king's writs, charters, etc. which entrench upon the weal of the people may be abrogated, nulled and made void by the parliament — the representative body of the land — and his very prerogatives bounded, restrained and limited by them, much more may the orders, warrants, commitments etc. of the Lords, with their usurped prerogatives over the Commons and people of England be restrained, nulled and made void by them. And therefore these lords must needs be inferior to them.

Further, the legislative power is not in the king himself but only in the kingdom and body representative, who has power to make or to abrogate laws, statutes etc. even without the king's consent. For by law he has not a negative voice either in making or reversing, but by his own coronation oath he is sworn 'to grant, fulfil, and defend all rightful laws, which the Commons of the realm shall choose, and to strengthen and maintain them after his power'; by which clause of the oath is evident that the Commons (not the king or Lords) have power to choose what laws themselves shall judge meetest, and thereto of necessity the king must assent. And this is evident by most of our former kings and parliaments, and especially by the reigns of the Edwards I to IV,

Richard II and the Henrys IV to VI. So that it cannot be denied but that the king is subordinate and inferior to the whole kingdom and body representative. Therefore if the king, much more must the lords veil their bonnets to the Commons and may not be esteemed the Upper House, or supreme court of judicature of the land.

So that seeing the sovereign power is not originally in the king, or personally terminated in him, then the king at most can be but chief officer or supreme executioner of the laws, under whom all other legal executioners, their several executions, functions and offices are subordinate; for indeed the representers (in whom that power is inherent and from whence it takes its original) can only make conveyance thereof to their representers, vicegerents or deputies, and cannot possibly further extend it. For so they should go beyond themselves, which is impossible, for *ultra posse non est esse*: there is no being beyond the power of being. That which goes beyond the substance and shadow of a thing cannot possibly be the thing itself either substantially or virtually; for that which is beyond the representers is not representative, and so not the kingdom's or people's, either so much as in shadow or substance.

Therefore the sovereign power, extending no further than from the represented to the representers — all this kind of sovereignty challenged by any (whether of king, Lords or others) is usurpation, illegitimate and illegal, and none of the kingdom's or people's. Neither are the people thereto obliged. Thus (sir) seeing the sovereign or legislative power is only from the represented to the representers, and cannot possibly legally further extend, the power of the king cannot be legislative but only executive, and he can communicate no more than he has himself. And the sovereign power not being inherent in him, it cannot be conveyed by or derived from him to any; for could he, he would have carried it away with him when he left the parliament. So that his mere prerogative creatures cannot have that which their lord and creator never had, has, or can have: namely, the legislative power. For it is a standing rule in nature, *omne simile generas simile*: every like begets its like. And indeed they are as like him as if they were spit out of his mouth.

For their proper station will not content them, but they must make incursions and inroads upon the people's rights and freedoms and extend their prerogative patent beyond their master's compass. Indeed all other courts might as well challenge that prerogative of sovereignty, yea better, than this court of lords. But and if any court or courts in this kingdom should arrogate to themselves that dignity to be the supreme court of judicatory of the land, it would be judged no less than high treason, to wit, for an inferior subordinate power to advance and exalt itself above the power of the parliament.

And (sir) the oppressions, usurpations, and miseries from this prerogative head are not the sole cause of our grievance and complaint, but in especial, the most unnatural, tyrannical, blood-thirsty desires and continual endeavours of the clergy against the contrary-minded in matters of conscience — which have been so veiled, gilded and covered over with such various, fair and specious pretences that by the common discernings such wolfish, cannibal, inhuman intents against their neighbours, kindred, friends and countrymen, as is now clearly discovered was little suspected (and less deserved) at their hands. But now I suppose they will scarce hereafter be so hard of belief. For now in plain terms and with open face, the clergy here discover themselves in their kind, and show plainly that inwardly they are no other but ravening wolves, even as roaring lions wanting their prey, going up and down, seeking whom they may devour.

For (sir) it seems these cruel minded men to their brethren, have, by the powerful agitation of Mr Tate and Mr Bacon (two members of the House) procured a most Romish inquisition ordinance to obtain an admission into the House, there to be twice read, and to be referred to a committee, which is of such a nature, if it should be but confirmed, enacted and established, as would draw all the innocent blood of the saints from righteous Abel unto this present upon this nation and fill the land with more martyrdoms, tyrannies, cruelties and oppressions than ever was in the bloody days of Queen Mary, yea or ever before, or since. For I may boldly say that the people of this nation never heard of such a diabolical, murdering, devouring ordinance, order, edict or law in their land as is that.

So that it may be truly said unto England: 'Woe to the inhabitants thereof, for the devil is come down unto you (in the shape of the letter B.) having great wrath, because he knows he has but a short time.' For never before was the like heard of in England. The cruel, villainous, barbarous martyrdoms, murders and butcheries of God's people under the papal and episcopal clergy were not perpetrated or acted by any law so devilish, cruel and inhumane as this. Therefore what may the free people of England expect at the hands of their Presbyterian clergy, who thus discover themselves more fierce and cruel than their fellows? Nothing but hanging, burning, branding, imprisoning, etc. is like to be the reward of the most faithful friends to the kingdom and parliament if the clergy may be the disposers — notwithstanding their constant magnanimity, fidelity and good service both in the field and at home, for them and the state.

But sure this ordinance was never intended to pay the soldiers; their arrears if it be, the Independents are like to have the best share, let them take that for their comfort. But I believe there was more tithe-providence than state-thrift in the matter; for if the Independents, Anabaptists, and Brownists were but sincerely addicted to the due payment of tithes, it would be better to them in this case than two-subsidy-men to acquit them of felony.

For were it not for the loss of their trade and spoiling their custom, an Anabaptist, Brownist, Independent and Presbyter were all one to them; then might they without doubt have the mercy of the clergy; then would they not have been entered into their Spanish Inquisition Calendar for absolute felons, or need they have feared the popish soul-murdering, anti-Christian Oath of Abjuration, or branding in the left cheek with the letter B — the new Presbyterian mark of the beast: for you see the devil is now again entered amongst us in a new shape, not like an angel of light (as both he and his servants can transform themselves when they please)but even in the shape of the letter B. From the power of which Presbyterian Beelzebub, good Lord deliver us all and let all the people say Amen. Then needed they not to have feared their prisons, their fire and faggot, their gallows and halters, etc. (the strongest texts in all the Presbyterian new model of clergy divinity for the maintenance and reverence of their cloth, and confutation of errors). For he that doth but so much as question that priest-fattening ordinance for tithes, oblations, obventions, etc. doth flatly deny the fundamentals of Presbytery, for it was the first stone they laid in their building; and the second stone was the prohibition of all to teach God's word but themselves — and so are *ipso facto* all felons etc.

By this (sir) you may see what bloody-minded men those of the black Presbytery be: what little love, patience, meekness, longsuffering and forbearance they have to their brethren. Neither do they as they would be done to or do to others as is done to them. For they would not be so served themselves of the Independents, neither have the Independents ever sought or desired any such things upon them, but would bear with them in all brotherly love if they would be but contented to live peaceably and neighbourly by them, and not thus to brand, hang, judge and condemn all for felons that are not like themselves. Sure (sir) you cannot take this murdering, bloody disposition of theirs for the spirit of Christianity; for Christian charity 'suffers long, is kind, envieth not, exalteth not itself, seeketh not its own, is not easily provoked, thinketh no evil, beareth all things, believeth all things, hopeth all things, endureth all things'. But these their desires and endeavours are directly contrary.

Therefore (sir) if you should suffer this bloody inroad of martyrdom, cruelties and tyrannies upon the free commoners of England with whose weal you are betrusted; if you should be so inhumane, undutiful, yea and unnatural unto us, our innocent blood will be upon you, and all the blood of the righteous that shall be shed by this ordinance, and you will be branded to future generations for England's Bloody Parliament.

If you will not think upon us, think upon your posterities. For I cannot suppose that any one of you would have your children hanged in case they should prove Independents, Anabaptists, Brownists — I cannot judge you so unnatural and inhumane to your own children. Therefore (sir) if for our own sakes we shall not be protected, save us for your children's sakes (though you think yourselves secure). For ye may be assured their and our interest is interwoven in one; if we perish, they must not think to escape. And (sir) consider that the cruelties, tyrannies and martyrdoms of the papal and episcopal clergy was one of the greatest instigations to this most unnatural war; and think you, if you settle a worse foundation of cruelty, that future generations will not taste of the dregs of that bitter cup?

Therefore now step in or never, and discharge your duties to God and to us and tell us no longer that such motions are not yet 'seasonable and we must still wait'; for have we not waited on your pleasures many fair seasons and precious occasions and opportunities these six years, even till the halters are ready to be tied to the gallows, and now must we hold our peace and wait till we be all imprisoned, hanged, burnt and confounded?

Blame us not (sir) if we complain against you — speak, write and plead thus with might and main — for our lives, laws and liberties; for they are our earthly *summum bonum*, wherewith you are chiefly betrusted, and whereof we desire a faithful discharge at your hands in especial. Therefore be not you the men that shall betray the blood of us and our posterities into the hands of those bloody black executioners. For God is just and will avenge our blood at your hands. And let heaven and earth bear witness against you, that for this end, that we might be preserved and restored, we have discharged our duties to you — both of love, fidelity and assistance and in what else ye could demand or devise in all your several needs, necessities and extremities — not thinking our lives, estates, nor anything too precious to sacrifice for you and the kingdom's safety. And shall we now be thus unfaithfully, undutifully and ungratefully rewarded? For shame let never such things be spoken, far less recorded, to future generations.

Thus sir, I have so far emboldened myself with you, hoping you will let grievances be uttered (that if God see it good they may be redressed), and give losers leave to speak without offence as I am forced to at this time, not only in the discharge of my duty to myself in particular but to yourselves and to our whole country in general for the present and for our several posterities for the future. And the Lord give you grace to take this timely advice from so mean and unworthy an instrument.

One thing more (sir) I shall be bold to crave at your hands: that you would be pleased to present my appeal, here enclosed, to your honourable House. Perchance the manner of it may beget a disaffection in you or at least a suspicion of disfavour from the House. But howsoever I beseech you that you would make presentation thereof, and if any hazard and danger ensue let it fall upon me; for I have cast up mine accounts. I know the most that it can cost me is but the dissolution of this fading mortality, which once must be dissolved; but after — blessed be God — comes righteous judgement.

Thus (sir) hoping my earnest and fervent desires after the universal freedoms and properties of this nation in general, and especially of the most godly and faithful in their consciences, persons and estates, will be a sufficient excuse with you for this my tedious presumption upon your patience, I shall commit the premises to your deliberate thoughts — and the issue thereof unto God, expecting and praying for His blessing upon all your faithful and honest endeavours in the prosecution thereof. And rest,

From the most contemptuous gaol of Newgate (the Lords' benediction)

25 September 1646

In bonds for the just rights and freedoms of the Commons of England, theirs and your faithful friend and servant, Richard Overton

To the high and mighty states, the knights, citizens and burgesses in parliament assembled (England's legal sovereign power). The humble appeal and supplication of Richard Overton, prisoner in the most contemptible gaol of Newgate.

Humbly shows,

That whereas your petitioner, under the pretence of a criminal fact being in a warlike manner brought before the House of Lords to be tried, and by them put to answer to interrogatories concerning himself — both which your petitioner humbly conceives to be illegal, and contrary to the natural rights, freedoms and properties of the free commoners of England (confirmed to them by Magna Carta, the Petition of Right and the Act for the abolishment of the Star Chamber) — he therefore was emboldened to refuse subjection to the said House both in the one and the other, expressing his resolution before them that he would not infringe the private rights and properties of himself or of any one commoner in particular, or the common rights and properties of this nation in general. For which your petitioner was by them adjudged contemptuous, and by an order from the said House was therefore committed to the gaol of Newgate, where, from the 11 of August 1646 to this present he has lain, and there commanded to be kept till their pleasures shall be further signified (as a copy of the said order hereunto annexed doth declare) which may be perpetual if they please, and may have their wills. For your petitioner humbly conceives as hereby he is made a prisoner to their wills, not to the law — except their wills may be a law.

Wherefore your liege petitioner doth make his humble appeal unto this most sovereign House (as to the highest court of judicatory in the land, wherein all the appeals thereof are to centre and beyond which none can legally be made) humbly craving (both in testimony of his acknowledgement of its legal regality and of his due submission thereunto) that your honours therein assembled would take his cause (and in his, the cause of all the free commoners of England, whom you represent and for whom you sit) into your serious consideration and legal determination, that he may either by the mercy of the law be repossessed of his just liberty and freedoms — and thereby the whole commons of England of theirs, thus unjustly (as he humbly conceives) usurped and invaded by the House of Lords — with due reparations of all such damages to sustained, or else that he may undergo what penalty shall in equity by the impartial severity of the law be adjudged against him by this honourable House in case by them he shall be legally found a transgressor herein.

And your petitioner (as in duty bound) shall ever pray, etc.

Die martis 11 *Augusti,* 1646

It is this day ordered by the Lords in parliament assembled, that Overton, brought before a committee of this House for printing scandalous things against this House, is hereby committed to the prison of Newgate for his high contempt offered to this House and to the said committee by his contemptuous words and gesture, and refusing to answer unto the Speaker. And that the said Overton shall be kept in safe custody by the Keeper of Newgate or his deputy until the pleasure of the House be further signified.

To the Gentleman Usher attending this House, or his deputy, to be delivered to the Keeper of Newgate or his deputy.

John Brown *Cleric. Parl. Examinat. per* Ra. Brisco *Clericu. de Newgate*

Postscript

Sir,

Your unseasonable absence from the House, chiefly while Mistress Lilburne's petition should have been read (you having a report to make in her husband's behalf whereby the hearing thereof was deferred and retarded) did possess my mind with strong jealousies and fears of you that you either preferred your own pleasure or private interest before the execution of justice and judgement, or else withdrew yourself on set purpose (through the strong instigation of the Lords) to evade the discharge of your trust to God and to your country. But at your return, understanding that you honestly and faithfully did redeem your absent time, I was dispossessed of those fears and jealousies. So that for my over-hasty censorious esteem of you I humbly crave your excuse, hoping you will rather impute it to the fervency of my faithful zeal to the common good than to any malignant disposition or disaffection in me towards you. Yet (sir) in this my suspicion I was not single, for it was even become a general surmise.

Wherefore (sir) for the awarding your innocency for the future from the tincture of such unjust and calumnious suspicions, be you diligent and faithful, instant in season and out of season; omit no opportunity (though with never so much hazard to your person, estate or family) to discharge the great trust in you reposed, with the rest of your fellow members, for the redemption of your native country from the arbitrary domination and usurpations, either of the House of Lords or any other.

And since by the divine providence of God it has pleased that honourable assembly whereof you are a member to select and sever you out from amongst themselves to be of that committee which they have ordained to receive the commoners' complaints against the House of Lords granted upon the foresaid most honourable petition, be you therefore impartial and just, active and resolute, care neither for favours nor smiles, and be no respecter of persons. Let not the greatest peers in the land be more respected with you than so many old bellows-menders, broom-men, cobblers, tinkers, or chimney-sweepers, who are all equally freeborn with the hugest men and loftiest Anakims in the land.

Do nothing for favour of the one or fear of the other. And have a care of the temporary sagacity of the new sect of opportunity politicians, whereof we have got at least two or three too many. For delays and demurrers of justice are of more deceitful and dangerous consequence than the flat and open denial of its execution; for the one keeps in suspense, makes negligent and remiss, the other provokes to speedy defence, makes active and resolute. Therefore be wise, quick, stout and impartial: neither spare, favour, or connive at friend or foe, high or low, rich or poor, lord or commoner.

And let even the saying of the Lord, with which I will close this present discourse, close with your heart and be with you to the death. Leviticus 19:15. 'Ye shall do no unrighteousness in judgement: thou shall not respect the person of the poor, nor honour the person of the mighty, but in righteousness shalt thou judge thy neighbour.'

12 October 1646

Note On This Edition

This edition was specially conceived and printed to accompany the publication of *How To Be A Liberal* by Ian Dunt. It reproduces the text of Richard Overton's *An Arrow Against All Tyrants* in its entirety from a copy at the British Library (shelfmark E.356[14]), but with some enhancements to make it more easily understood by 21st Century readers.

Rather than use the fold-out DIY design of the original 20-page pamphlet, we have printed it in book form, and used modern spellings. To elaborate on the circumstances of *An Arrow*'s original publication in the 1640s, Canbury Press commissioned an expert in 17th Century print culture, Ian Gadd, Professor of English Literature at Bath Spa University, to write an introduction, for which he has our thanks.

Canbury Press publishes high-quality non-fiction: our other books are a little more up-to-date. You can find out more at canburypress.com.

Martin Hickman
Managing Director
Canbury Press

www.canburypress.com
Telling the real story since 2013